Xenophobe's®
guide to the
CZECHS

Petr Berka
Aleš Palán
Petr Šťastný

Oval Books

Published by Oval Books, London

Telephone: +44 (0)20 7733 8585
E-mail: info@ovalbooks.com
Web site: www.ovalbooks.com

First printed 2008, reprinted 2009

Editor – Catriona Tulloch Scott
Series Editor – Anne Tauté

Cover designer – Vicki Towers
Printer – J.F. Print Ltd., Sparkford, Somerset
Producer – Oval Projects Ltd.

Thanks are given to Benjamin Kuras for his kind
permission to quote passages from his book
Czechs and Balances: A Nation's Survival Guide,
published by Baronet, Prague; and to Petr Šťastný
for the silhouette of Prague and the map.

Cover: garnets which embody the Czech Republic's
tradition of glass jewellery-making.

This book is stocked in the Czech Republic by:
Big Ben Novelties Ltd, Prague.
Telephone: + 420 603 832 056

Xenophobe's® is a Registered Trademark.

ISBN: 978-1-902825-23-6

Contents

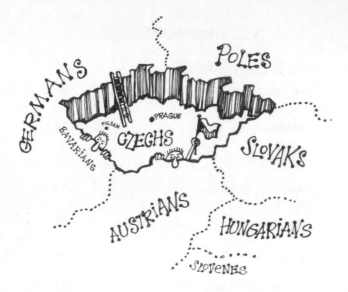

The population of the Czech Republic is 10 million compared with around 5 million Slovaks, 8 million Austrians, 10 million Hungarians, 38.5 million Poles, 62 million British, 82 million Germans, 141 million Russians and 301 million Americans.

The Czech Republic is nearly twice the size of Switzerland, a third bigger than its former partner Slovakia, and a bit smaller than either Austria or Ireland. On the other hand, it could fit into Poland very nearly 4 times.

Nationalism & Identity

A land with no name

The Czechs have no one-word term to denote their homeland.

Within the territory of the Czech basin – which is essentially a hilly countryside surrounded by marginally higher mountains – an important feudal domain evolved. It was called the Czech Kingdom. Not long ago, Czechs lived in a joint state with the Slovaks. That state was known as Czechoslovakia. Today, a democratic system is to be found here. Its name is the Czech Republic. The Czechs, therefore, can express their homeland using either an adjective, 'Czech', or in compounds; the noun is simply missing.

There is in existence the name 'Čechy' (sometimes translated as Bohemia), but that refers only to the western part of the country, while the eastern part is called Moravia. Czech journalists have a tendency to use the neologism Czechia (Česko), but barring nothing short of a linguistic miracle, the Czechs will forever have to be content with merely an adjective for their nation. It must simply be good enough for them to live in a Republic, which is Czech.

> **66 The Czechs will forever have to be content with merely an adjective for their nation. 99**

1

National pride

National pride is only usually demonstrated in sport. The only time Czechs sing their national anthem is after winning a match. People rarely react when it is played on the radio or TV, they just carry on as normal. The national anthem was not even composed as an official song. It was originally a 19th-century song from a comedy about a shoemaker's holiday, the name of which is 'Where is my home?'

> **❝ The Czechs seem to believe that the Earth is the centre of the Universe, Europe is the centre of the Earth and Czechia is at the centre of Europe. ❞**

In the 16th century, Copernicus pointed out that the Sun, not the Earth, is the centre of the solar system, a fact that appears to have passed way over the heads of the Czechs. They seem to believe to this day that the Earth is at the centre of the Universe. And that, if the Earth is the centre of the Universe, Europe is the centre of the Earth and Czechia is at the centre of Europe.

The Czech Republic does in fact lie roughly at the centre of this Continent; all it takes is a look at the map, bearing in mind that the eastern borders of Europe are not formed by the suburbs of Munich but by the Urals at the borders of Siberia. It follows then, that Czechia is indeed the absolute centre of the Universe.

Hardly a year passes without some village or other

claiming, on the basis of computing with the aid of a school atlas, a ruler and a cheap calculator bought for one Euro at the stationery shop, that it, and it alone, is in the exact geometrical centre of Czechia, and consequently the centre of the Universe. A small flaw in these claims is the sheer number of them: there are roughly 80, and the number is growing.

How they see themselves

A Czech sees himself as the hero of a novel. Not, however, a psychologically torn, post-modern hero from the novels of the Czech author Milan Kundera. Not even the hero warrior from old Czech legends. But a good-hearted, easy-going figure, somewhat rotund, talkative, garrulous even,

> **A Czech sees himself as the hero of a novel... This hero is the good old soldier Švejk.**

who indulges in beer and pickled sausages (a local delicacy nicknamed '*utopence*', which translates as 'sinkers' or 'drowned people'). This hero is the good old soldier Švejk.

Švejk, though a soldier, is essentially anti-militarist. All the same, he is drafted into the First World War and there he proves to be so idiotic and incompetent as to become a totally useless cog in the war machine. Although he is absolved from military service on an evaluation of his IQ, totally stupid he is not. In Czech pubs and in lecture theatres alike, even 80 or more years after the publication of the book, a lively discussion about whether Švejk is a real idiot or successfully pretending to be one, rages on. In any case, he proves himself to be more sensible than all the blood-thirsty warmongers around him.

Švejk is an inconspicuous Czech fellow. With a ready smile and silver tongue, he slips with almost proverbial luck from any scrimmage. He is a permanent outsider, but he knows how to live life to the full. He cannot be sad for long. While other national opuses trumpet the idea of love (truth, honour, etc.) being stronger than death, Švejk claims that virtue also lies in a jolly mind, endless tall tales, a certain degree of shallowness and limitless determination not to get involved in any situation. Švejk is not a participant in history, he is its saboteur. For his ability to sail through life the term 'švejking' has been coined.

> **Virtue lies in a jolly mind, endless tall tales, a certain degree of shallowness and limitless determination not to get involved in any situation.**

Every Czech is a bit like Švejk. A Czech who reads Jaroslav Hašek's *The Good Soldier Švejk and His Fortunes in the World War* is looking in the mirror. And he looks with satisfaction, like a prima donna trying on a new necklace before the ball.

Švejking carries within itself one great frustration.

The inability to be a driving force of history and inseminator of ideas to redeem mankind becomes some form of general sociological retardation. In short the Czechs suffer from the classic inferiority complex of a small nation.

There are 10 million Czechs, and other similarly large (a Czech will say small) nations would refer to themselves as medium sized. If Hungarians, Portuguese or Swedes are small, what would Luxemburgers be? Or the inhabitants of San Marino? But the Czechs consider themselves to be small. They rate their own character as dove-like. In history the Czechs were always the innocent invaded ones – here from the west, there from the east – while all they ever wanted to do was to invent, write poetry and just be themselves. The invaders stole the drawings and plans, exploited them and from then on passed them off as their own. Thus, very few inventions managed to get smuggled all the way to the patent office by Czech chaps. For example, the Veverka cousins undoubtedly invented something called the '*ruchadlo*' – an obscure improvement to the common plough. The world was supposed to sit up in awe.

> **The Czechs rate their own character as dove-like. In history they were always the innocent invaded ones.**

This story is a part of the nation's primary school curriculum and every small child knows it by heart. It is a wonder that the birthdates of the learned cousins have not yet been proclaimed a national holiday. (To be sure it would be a very popular one, for in this case it would have to be two days.)

The Czechs are extremely proud of their *ruchadlo*. The fact that nobody really knows exactly what a *ruchadlo* is, and what it's good for, does not change anything one iota.

> **66 They wonder why the CNN news service does not offer a regular daily rubric: Good News from Czechia. 99**

The Czechs feel they would easily excel over other nations, if only first Vienna, then Berlin and Moscow and now Brussels would not hinder them. So they stand somewhat pushed aside and they wonder why the CNN news service does not offer a regular daily rubric: Good News from Czechia. It is clearly an injustice and a shameful omission, but the Czechs – the Švejks – are taking it bravely.

Despite all this, the Czechs consider they have among them the biggest personality of all mankind, Jára Cimrman, the most colossally intelligent multi-inventor and mega-creator. This fictional character of non-existent genius was born a few years ago in one of Prague's theatres. His persona, however, recently stepped down from stage and entered the real, almost political, world, when in a national TV poll Jára Cimrman was voted with a landslide majority as the greatest ever Czech. The organizers were reluctant to announce a non-existent figure as the overall winner of a poll in which in Britain, for example, Winston Churchill took the lead. For this reason they had the poor Cimrman disqualified and the declared winner was the medieval monarch, King Charles IV. The Czechs simply '*švejked*' the poll; they wouldn't have it any other way.

How they feel about their neighbours

The Czechs were twice occupied in the 20th century, the first time by the Germans (1938-1945) and the second time by the Soviets (1968-1990). After the Second World War, the Czechs had the three-million-strong German population removed from Czech lands (what the Germans called the Sudetenland), or rather from Czechia, actually the then Czechoslovakia... you see the confusion caused by a missing noun, and still to this day they harbour the delusion of being the victors in this age-old neighbourly dispute. They look therefore at German tourists with a mixture of

> **66 They are fully aware of the economic potential of their western neighbour – a potential they hope to find in the visitors' wallets. 99**

condescension and envy. They are fully aware of the economic potential of their western neighbour – a potential which they hope to find a small part of in the visitors' wallets.

To be a German is not a crime in the Czech Republic anymore. However a citizen of that nation must reckon with being viewed, regardless of his true character, as an unsympathetic, coarse and bigheaded creature, devoid of even the most elementary sense of humour.

All traditional German virtues – a sense of comradeship, orderliness, dutifulness, obedience and so forth – are to Czechs almost a complete list of human depravities.

> **66 All traditional German virtues – a sense of comradeship, orderliness, dutifulness, obedience and so forth – are to Czechs almost a complete list of human depravities. 99**

Surprisingly, Germans are not the victims of Czech jokes all that often. When Czechs are poking fun at someone, it's usually the super-powers such as the Americans, the Russians or the Martians. Only these are worthy of comparison.

The Czech term for Germans originated from the adjective 'dumb'. The ancient Czechs simply could not understand the ancient Germans and thus, with perfectly sound logic, concluded that Germans can't talk. To be dumb is a time-honoured and well-proven formula for the safe survival of a German in Czechia. The Czechs are much more, in fact really very much more, tolerant towards the dumb.

The Czechs have a complex about the Germans because they seem to be more successful at almost everything, and more and more German companies are arriving in their midst. Many people worry that their country will be sold out to the Germans and what Germany didn't achieve with their army they will do with their money. The Czechs are only able to beat the Germans at three things:

1) beer drinking,
2) ice hockey, and
3) being on the right side during world wars.

Czechs don't find German women attractive; they feel (along with Jára Cimrman) that it's 'Better to have a warm Czech beer than a cold German woman'.

To the south of the Czech border lies Austria whose inhabitants have the indisputably bad luck to be German-speaking too. They are pardoned though, mainly thanks to the fact of being less numerous than Germans and therefore attracting fewer reservations. But Austrians did not endear themselves to many Czechs when, after the lifting of the Iron Curtain, they put up in their shops insulting notices: 'Czechs, don't steal!' One half of the nation felt insulted by this wild accusation, while the other half mused over how the Austrians could have found out.

Historically, the Poles were always viewed as horse-traders, pedlars and thieves, the Hungarians were

> **❝Czechs feel that it's 'Better to have a warm Czech beer than a cold German woman.'❞**

primitive vegetable farmers and probably thieves, the Romanians, Bulgarians and Yugoslavs were child snatchers, smugglers and definitely thieves. The Russians and Ukrainians were unmentionables. This distorted image sticks and has a lot to do with the still bitter memory of some of these countries having taken a part in the Soviet-led invasion that put a brutal end to the so-called 'Prague Spring', the Czechs' noble and naive attempt at reforms. (It tends to be forgotten that Romania refused to send soldiers to assist the Soviets, and Yugoslavia even offered the Czechs and Slovaks military aid.)

> 66 As for the Byelorussians and Moldavians who work in his country, to a Czech they all blend into one post-Soviet stew. 99

As for the Byelorussians and Moldavians who work in his country, to a Czech they all blend into one post-Soviet stew. He is quite sure about one thing, that their work for next-to-nothing on building sites is only a sham. In reality they are all mafia.

Today, as the *zloty* climbs upwards, Czechs claim all Poles to be black-market racketeers. This criticism, however, does not prevent the cheap street markets of Polish border towns from being chock-a-block every weekend with eager Czech shoppers.

On the other hand the Vietnamese, who have lived in the country since the communist regime as part of a brotherly socialistic barter trade (to Vietnam flowed

Czech arms and machinery, back to Europe as a reward travelled Vietnamese students, though how this could have been profitable nobody understands even today), have established themselves and proved to be excellent businessmen and traders. By and large they peddle total rubbish which really should have been banned by the authorities. The Czechs know what they are talking about: a Vietnamese digital watch or a colourful set of plastic plates is to be found in every Czech household.

Special relationships
Positive:

The most amicably accepted nationals are the Slovaks. The Czechs have even pardoned them for disaffiliating themselves from the Czechs after decades of co-existence. With the patronising attitude of an older brother, the Czechs tell the Slovaks – whose economy is much more progressive than that of Czechia – how to do things, and are offended when the Slovaks do things differently. But they always forgive them. Czechs and Slovaks really do seem to be brothers. Their languages are so similar that members of both nations easily understand each other. To the

> **With the patronising attitude of an older brother, the Czechs tell the Slovaks how to do things, and are offended when the Slovaks do things differently.**

Czechs, who don't really master any foreign language, it gives the elated feeling of true worldliness.

The question then is why, when they are so alike, were they not able to continue to live together within the one state of Czechoslovakia? Most people would tell you it was a political and economic decision made by Parliament, or that two nations should live in two states. The country was divided without a referendum at a time when most Czechs and Slovaks didn't actually want it. They were happy together in Czechoslovakia and they are happy separated in two states. No wonder then that Czech and Slovak experts were invited to Belgium and Canada to advise them about a contingent separation.

> **" The country was divided without a referendum at a time when most Czechs and Slovaks didn't actually want it. "**

If you need a divorce of this sort and you don't know how it should be done, the logical thing is to consult the Czechs and Slovaks. And then hope your wife or husband will be as easy-going about it as they were.

Special relationships
Negative:
There is one other nation, a nation within the nation, right on the doorstep of nearly every Czech town or

village – the Romanies. There is an unknown number of them, and political correctness dictates that nobody does the count. It is also unacceptable to use the word 'gypsy' – the only exception being a popular traditional type of sausage called 'the gypsy'. The Czechs would rather have a German than a '*Roma*' for a neighbour. Romanies are considered lazy (even more than Poles), loud (even more than Germans) and crafty (even more than Czechs) – a really toxic combination.

> **"There is an unknown number of Romanies and political correctness dictates that nobody does the count. "**

The butt-end of Czech jokes used to be the Russians, the communist police and the Slovaks. With the demise of communism, and the Slovaks now independent, this type of humour has lost its lustre and it's the Czech gypsies with their numerous children, their 'light fingers', and their milking of the social system that have taken their place. For instance:

> An unemployed gypsy pays a reluctant visit to the employment office and says 'I want work, I want a job.' The clerk looks at him in astonishment and offers him a super executive position with a huge salary, his own office, a company limousine and a dishy secretary. The shocked gypsy shouts angrily 'Are you taking the mickey!?' 'Yes I am,' says the clerk, 'but you started it.'

How others see them

The Czechs know only too well how others see them for hardly a week goes by without the results of yet another research project among tourists being published. To be obsessed with your own image is typical not only of adolescent teenagers, but of young nations too.

For the Germans, Czechs have always been part of their expansion towards the east. The Charles University in Prague is considered by many Germans to be the oldest *German* university. At the turn of the 18th and 19th centuries most of the Czechs spoke only German. According to the Germans, Czechs were the

66 The Germans believe that Czechs are very skilled, but in need of management. 99

labourers in the Czech Kingdom and the Germans the lords. And they still believe it to be the case nowadays that Czechs should work in the factories built after the end of communism by German companies.

The Germans believe that Czechs are very skilled, but in need of management. With good (in other words German) management the country will flourish. In Germany the expression 'a Czech village' means a dirty, disorganised place. They think that's how the Czechs would end up without the Germans.

A lot of Russians come to Prague and to the spa town Karlovy Vary. They find Czechs narrow-minded; they say Prague is a beautiful city, but small. They think Becherovka (a Czech tipple) is interesting, but unfortunately not as strong as their vodka.

The Austrians feel they have a special relationship with the Czechs. For more than three centuries the Czech Kingdom was part of the Habsburg Empire with its capital in Vienna. At the end of the 19th century there were more Czechs living in Vienna than in Prague, and the Austrians say that every Viennese person has at least one Czech grandmother.

> **Deep down, Austrians and Czechs consider one another's nation as the worst in the world.**

But deep down, Austrians and Czechs cannot stand each other; they consider one another's nation to be the worst in the world. Never admit to either of them that you think they are similar as they would be deeply insulted. When they look at one another it is like looking into a mirror and seeing all their own mistakes.

How they would like to be seen

They would like to be seen as a modern, rapidly developing country full of promise, opportunities and educated people; as being not only the link between the West and East, but also the cauldron in which all that's good from West and East melts; as, if not *the* best, then at least one of the top nations in the world.

For starters, Czechs consider that they have the

best cuisine and the best beer in the galaxy (Bohemian dumplings and Pilsen Urquell being the super-stars), the prettiest girls (Dolly Buster, Ivana Trump, Eva Herzigova to mention just a few), the best sportsmen since the stone age (Zátopek, Navrátilová, Lendl, Jágr, Nedvěd), and one of the world's great actors, Herbert Lom (Inspector Clouseau's put-upon Chief of Police).

66 **The Czechs would like to be seen as the cauldron in which all that's good from West and East melts; as if not the best, then at least one of the top nations in the world.** 99

To which can be added a belief of the Czechs that they are a sophisticated nation with the oldest education institution in the world – the Charles University, 1348 (in reality the 20th oldest); the finest artists, philosophers, writers, poets and thinkers – Havel, Kafka, Kundera, Forman, Čapek, Hašek, Seifert, Comenius (a 16th-century champion of universal education); businessmen and inventors – Škoda, Baťa, Wichterle (the father of soft contact lenses), Heyrovský (Nobel prize-winning chemist), musicians and composers – Dvořák, Smetana, Janáček. According to some, the only real danger to any listener is that the list is almost limitless.

All in all, the Czechs want the outside world to be like them. This is also the official result of a poll conducted by a leading national broadsheet. The question put to the public was: 'If you had to choose

16

another country to live in, where would it be?' To everyone's surprise the answer was not Tahiti, Paris, Dubai, the Seychelles or Florida, but Slovakia.

Why?

Because, as a former part of the country it is the closest everyone can get to their most admired, desired and loved nation in the universe – the Czechs.

Character

A state of fed-upness

This trait is the first thing that a foreigner will notice after arrival at the airport, train or coach station. The surly Customs officer frowns at you and you are afraid that he probably knows about the contraband chewing-gum in your suit-case. The receptionist in the hotel glowers at you and you get the impression that she had her own plans about what to do with your booked room that evening. The sales assistant in the shop looks so glum that you want to ask her if her much-loved cat has died. It has not. She just looks like that. While members of other ethnicities need to have a serious reason for being sullen, the Czechs need none.

> **While members of other ethnicities need to have a serious reason for being sullen, the Czechs need none.**

17

If you don't want to upset them, don't try to cheer them up. If you happen to travel on public transport and there is no escape until the next stop, you had better hide your smiling face and sparkling look behind a scarf or a hat. In the summer you can stare at the ground or try to imagine that you aren't on your way to a concert followed by a splendid supper, but to your dentist for an operation which you have been putting off for half a year.

Besides their gloomy mien, perpetual Czech grumpiness is expressed by endless complaints. Before the arrival of communism, Czechs lived in one of the richest countries in the world and they are slowly returning to that state. But they are still unhappy. It's just not happening fast enough for them. In comparison with the rest of the European Union, the Czech Republic has the least number of people threatened by poverty. Despite this, the inhabitants are fed up; it's not sufficient that nobody is really poor, they themselves are not rich enough.

> **The inhabitants are fed up; it's not sufficient that nobody is really poor, they themselves are not rich enough.**

Don't be afraid though, for they are quite harmless. It is just a typical look on their faces and is not usually accompanied by aggressive behaviour. The Czechs enjoy being teed-off. It is their most affordable hobby.

Passive passion

Throughout the centuries of suppression, Czechs have managed to save their national identity with relative ease. Their secret is not to revolt against the regime, but to wait, knowing that at some point the suppression will end without the need to fight. Under the Habsburg suppression they waited for 300 years; under the Nazi occupation they waited 7 years; under communism they waited 40 years: when Soviet tanks entered the country in 1968 hardly a man defended the country with gun in hand and eventually the Soviets and communists left anyway. Czechs are patient and they have time.

Occupying authorities have always been afraid of fake Czech loyalty. Reinhard Heydrich, the Reich protector until 1942, the so-called Butcher of Prague, said that the Czechs are much more dangerous than the Yugoslavs, who he described as being like a branch which breaks only with extreme effort. You can't break the Czechs because they are like willow cane: you can push them to the ground but they lash back when you least expect it. He was right. Only a few months after he said these words he was assassinated.

> **You can't break the Czechs because they are like willow cane… they lash back when you least expect it.**

Part of the mode of survival that the Czechs developed was to behave differently in private and in

19

public. At home they would say what they really believe (and raise their children along the same lines: "What you hear at home is to be kept at home, in public you agree with others"). In public, they would acquiesce with the authorities and do as they were told. However, more often than not, they not only did it, they overdid it. For example, with the order to decorate every building, house, window and roof in the land with red Soviet flags to mark the tediously numerous communist anniversaries, what would our little Czech do? He would also put one or two on the outside toilet of his country cottage.

Opportunists all

Cunning is a specifically Czech characteristic. It is masked by a variety of terms, most of them untranslatable. Basically it involves an artful, tricky craftiness – though with a certain degree of charm. For example: Czech town municipalities receive money from the state coffers according to their population figures. Small town, small money; big town, big money.

One smallish town during a population census realised that to reach the desired mark of 50,000 inhabitants it was short of some 200 souls. So it announced that any 'new' resident (which involved merely formal, paper residency, everybody remaining where they actually lived) would receive as a reward a nice little sum of money.

People were 'moving' in droves, but all in all the town paid out a few hundred thousand, and from the treasury it got a few million. The town hall behaved as a typical Czech would do: cunningly. It was a sham, but nobody was actually hurt, so while you may feel this is

> **Cunning is a specifically Czech characteristic... an artful, tricky craftiness – though with a certain degree of charm.**

wrong, to the Czechs it seems irresistibly crafty. And make no mistake: they will take the first opportunity to try something similar on you.

Knife-edge intelligence

Shrewdness of this kind is not the product of a mediocre mind. As has been pointed out in the highly acclaimed *Czechs and Balances*:

'The Czechs are fast learners and tend to remember what they learn for as long as it is usable, and sometimes long after it has become useless.

They have a deep desire and unwavering determination to better themselves – materially, intellectually, and culturally – whatever the circumstances, and through their own effort. Their aim is nothing less than being at the very top of the European league where they believe they belong and where they still vaguely recall having once been – economically, culturally and in whatever other area of competition they may consider relevant at a given time.'

What saves them from being quite unbearably astute is that: 'They have a unique knack for screwing up when it really matters. Which is why they are where they are, not where they know they ought to be.'

Reluctance to be self-reliant

The Czech film director Miloš Forman (*Hair, Amadeus, One Flew Over the Cuckoo's Nest*) has compared life under communism to existence in a zoo – there is usually plenty of food, medical care is provided, only freedom is in short supply. Conversely, Forman likened freedom to a jungle, where everybody must take care of himself.

66 Czechs are reluctant to take care of themselves: they believe institutions will do the job better than they could themselves. 99

Czechs are reluctant to take care of themselves: they believe they have been set up for the purpose of institutions, which will do the job better than they could themselves. Thus, to get a job is not up to the worker but up to the unions, employers or government; to achieve a satisfactory level of education is not the responsibility of the individual student, or his parents, but of the education system. Preventative health care is not a job for the

Czech patient but for his doctor. This reliance on the powers-that-be suggests a deep-seated political leftism; in fact it's more about the Czechs' fundamental belief that survival is given a better chance if you allow yourself to be directed.

A Czech is not an individualist, but neither is he a collectivist. He has an essential need to belong (whether to allotment or cremation associations or to the Christian Democrats), but within the framework of his domiciliary group he behaves in a most peculiar way. He does not attend meetings, moans about the regulations and pays his membership fees only after the second reminder, and then at the very last moment.

> **66 The Czech disturbs everybody around him with his chaotic state and unwillingness to accept discipline. 99**

He disturbs everybody around him not with his excessive individualism but rather with his chaotic state and unwillingness to accept discipline. But, as the Czechs say: 'Order befits only the idiot. The truly intelligent manages even chaos.'

Envy

There isn't an older Czech wheeze than this: God and Saint Peter were walking the Earth. It was a cold night and they were looking for a place to put their heads down. Everywhere they were refused, until they reached a dilapidated cottage where they were received with kindness and even with a share of simple food. God revealed himself and offered their hosts anything they could possibly wish for. "Lord, we have nothing but a pair of old hens, while our neighbour has a nice, young goat. Every day it gives them two litres of milk..." "You'd like the same?" interrupts God. "No," replies the villager. "We want their goat to die."

Czech society is egalitarian, but maintaining average levels is achieved not by the weaker individuals trying harder but, on the contrary, by the stronger ones getting desirably weaker. The average, then, is quite close to zero, but this is not what matters: the main thing is that nobody stands out. The fact that in spite of this tendency the Czech economy stays productive and the local culture flourishes could be best explained as proof of God's existence. Any natural explanation is missing.

> **Czech society is egalitarian, but maintaining average levels is achieved not by the weaker individuals trying harder but by the stronger ones getting desirably weaker.**

To be successful in Czechia is unforgivable – the real tycoons therefore wear tacky clothes and travel to their small ex-council flats by tram. School children envy each other's lice: the reason is understandable – the lousy ones don't need to go to school next day and on top of that could trade the vermin in their hair to their still uncontaminated mates for exorbitant sums. The Czechs are able to envy even your misfortune, as long as it's a big one.

There is an old Czech saying about a man who envies his fellow man's 'nose between his eyes'. You will be well advised not to laugh at this but rather feel your face. Have you still got yours?

National Obsessions

Cottages

Had the Surrealist André Breton ever visited certain regions of the Czech countryside he would have seen his dream realised: the surreal made real.

> **❝Imagine Tolkien's Hobbiton and you're about halfway there.❞**

Almost every Czech family has their own weekend cottage (mostly by inheritance from grandparents). The use of the term 'cottage' here should not conjure up images of quaint Alpine chalets; each Czech cottage is a unique creation, an absolute original, which describes and is moulded by the personality of its inhabitants. Imagine Tolkien's Hobbiton and you're about halfway there. Upon entering a typical Czech cottage, your first impression is likely to be that it is just about to fall down. You'd be mistaken. What you will have failed to take into account is the steel wire tied to the nearest tree, holding the roof on.

To truly understand Czech popular architecture, do not only look for it in the historic medieval town centres, but follow the swarms of Škodas out of the cities on Friday afternoon to the little hamlets of weekend cottages in the forest where people potter about in their cottages, mow the lawns and perhaps build a small corrugated iron outhouse or nail a few more sets of antlers to the wall. After a weekend of such feverish activity they return to the cities to relax, sit back and take it easy at their workplace in order to stock up on energy for the next weekend.

During communist times there were no opportunities for people to start private enterprise or to travel, so they channelled their efforts into these fantasies. Because of the lack of materials in the shops, they had to buy supplies on the black market or pilfer them from their place of work for themselves and their friends. No-one considered stealing from the state to be a crime, and a common expression was: 'Who doesn't steal from the state, steals from the family.'

Golden hands

The phenomenon of the Czech country cottage marries two great obsessions: on the one hand the romantic yearning for the countryside, the mountains and the forests, on the other, the basic instinct of Czech males to nail things together. The acute shortage of virtually everything in communist times forced the average citizen to master the art of improvisation – the much vaunted 'Czech Golden Hands' which implies that they are skillful and dexterous. It's a phrase that will be uttered by a plumber after he floods your bathroom or by a car mechanic who has forgotten to adjust the brakes of your car. And when you, with only the steering wheel in your hands, are trying to complain about his work, he won't accept your claim: don't you know that the Czechs have hands made of gold?

Regardless of one's profession, everybody had to learn to do whatever was needed. This is how the myth of the golden-handed Czech was born. And it still survives, even though times have changed and nowadays everything can be easily purchased, ready made. For the average Czech DIY fanatic this would be below his dignity. His golden hands can surely manage much better. The day they stop would be the Czech equivalent of the ravens leaving the Tower of London: the world would probably end.

> **Everybody had to learn to do whatever was needed. This is how the myth of the golden-handed Czech was born.**

Gardening

Not even one's garden is safe. For a Czech to get his hands dirty digging the soil (even for the extermination of a mole) brings a sense of delight to the soul comparable only to the first orgasm or the first successful tax-dodge of the financial year.

Home owners have made some great contributions to the world of horticulture. Old car tyres, painted and used as makeshift plant pots are an essential in any Czech garden. Ladders, too, have been found to be unnecessary; if a tree obstructs your view, simply chop off the tree as high as you can reach.

> **Rather than eating any produce while fresh, it is vastly preferable to boil, cook down, pickle or otherwise preserve it.**

Furthermore, no garden can be complete without some fruit or veg growing in it: a row of carrots is a particularly decorative choice. It has been discovered by generations of Czech gardeners that rather than eating any produce while fresh, it is vastly preferable to boil, cook down, pickle or otherwise preserve it. This can usefully be off-loaded on any visitors or distant relatives.

Collecting

Whatever can't be placed in or around one's cottage, planted in the garden, pickled or distilled, can have only one other use to a Czech: to be collected.

Collecting things, anything, is another great Czech obsession. Virtually anything can be collected and swapped. For example, a second division hockey puck is currently worth 17 stamps with a picture of a koala bear on them. Just beware the gentleman who claims to collect passports, and under no circumstances swap yours.

Slippers

Czechs love slippers. When you visit a Czech family, you take your shoes off at the front door and they offer you slippers. If they are too small, the father of the family might slip off his slippers and say: "You can wear mine, they're bigger." You can see office employees wearing a suit, and slippers. Several MPs wore them to work and finally the deputies decided to vote on this issue and a law was passed restricting slippers during parliamentary sessions.

Tramping

This guide for xenophobes naturally makes great use of hyperbole; it is unfortunate therefore that what follows will be rejected by many people as a total - fabrication. It is not. This really goes on in the Czech Republic every weekend.

The origins of this unusual pastime lie in the period

between the two World Wars when young people, dis-illusioned with reality, took to dressing up as Cowboys and Indians to act out a romantic vision of the American Wild West in the forests outside the cities. Like-minded Czechs soon found each other: one com-rade took a guitar, a second one a banjo and the third his sister and in no time the first tramp camp or *osada* (with such names as 'The Lost Hope' or 'Arizona') was formed.

To this day, every Friday after work, hundreds of Czech people, especially of the older generation, don their costumes (regardless of the weather) and head to the near-est forest. There, all weekend, they sit around campfires cook-ing *kabanos* (spicy sausages) on the flames and singing hope-lessly sentimental songs.

> **66 All weekend they sit around campfires cooking sausages on the flames and singing hopelessly sentimental songs. 99**

The typical tramp of today is about 65-years-old, weighs roughly 18 stone, can still only play three chords on his guitar and has never been further west than Pilsen. Don't, whatever you do, tell him that today there are skyscrapers, freeways and a space centre in Texas. It would destroy his fantasy, and he wouldn't believe you anyway.

Younger tramps don't look like frontiersmen or Indians any more. When you see a man in an army outfit with a military knapsack and a guitar over his shoulder, the chances are that it is not a deserter from the Czech Army, it's a tramp.

Hiking

Czechs with similar inclinations to tramping and without the means to buy their own little cabins in the woods turn their attention to hiking around the Czech countryside instead. Take the above portrait of your typical tramp and just substitute a raincoat for a hat with a fox's tail, a compass for the guitar, take away six stone, and there you have your typical Czech hiker.

Mushroom picking

In summer another popular weekend activity is to go mushroom picking. It might be encompassed in a visit to the family hut or it might be a totally separate trip. Many Czechs have their secret place rich in mushrooms deep within a forest. A large part of Czechia is covered in forests and all are open to the public. In order to go mushroom picking you will need the following: a big wicker basket, gumboots and a jack-knife.

> **The mushroom picker only tells the general area, never ever the exact place.**

And you have to get up very early, at around 4 a.m.

If, in the afternoon, when the mushroom pickers are on their way home from a hard day's picking, they meet other mushroom pickers, they will peer into each other's wicker baskets and try to discover where the mushrooms were found. The mushroom picker only tells the general area, never ever the exact place. That's top secret.

Wild mushrooms are eaten not only as a side dish, but as a main meal too. Nearly all Czechs can recognise dozens of sorts of mushrooms and you don't have to worry about them bringing poisonous ones home. If invited, don't be afraid to accept an offer to dine on some of the delectable mushroom dishes. There are, after all, only a few cases of mushroom poisoning per year.

Politics

If levels of obsession were measured in blood pressure, then politics would definitely rank as the Czech's number one national obsession. Everyone in the Republic knows enough about politics to be absolutely certain that they would make a better president or prime minister than the current one. In some countries people get their thrills from jumping off a bridge with a rubber band tied to their ankles. In the Czech Republic people get the same effects from heated political arguments. The most beautiful thing about it is that, without any consideration of political allegiance, everyone agrees about one

66 Czechs get their thrills from heated political arguments. 99

thing: that it's all wrong. It's enough to make one thoroughly fed up... And what else could bring a Czech more contentment than that?

Sense of Humour

The Czechs like betting. Not for large sums, but just for the fun of it. And you can bet that if you ask five Czechs what is the most important element in their national character at least four of them will say that it's a sense of humour.

A Czech can say about another Czech (or about Czechs in general) that they are envious, dependent

> **You should never, ever question a Czech's sense of humour.**

and extremely cunning. In specific cases he can state with impunity that someone is fat, lazy or smelly. It is even possible to insult a person with obscenities. But you should never, ever question a Czech's sense of humour. Even to hint that someone is a killjoy will whip him into an immediate, verbal, sometimes even physical, fury. (And if he kicks out three of your teeth, the jury will free him, for it will be judged that he acted with just cause.) On the other hand, to say that his mother is a notorious hooker will end at most with a pint of beer poured over your head. (The jury might even start digging up the real truth behind the accusation of low morals.)

Don't, however, have any illusions about the quality of Czech humour. One popular local comic (Jan Werich), who is taken for being witty and wise at the same time, said "humour is not about laughing, but about knowing". Real life limps on all fours behind this claim. A delicate smile, the mouth's corners slightly upturned – that's not humour for a Czech. On the contrary, real humour is distinguished by mad screams, breast and thigh slapping and uncontrollable braying.

> **❝Czech humour is distinguished by mad screams, breast and thigh slapping and uncontrollable braying.❞**

Franz Kafka, a man with a Czech surname who lived in Prague but was German speaking, loved a special kind of joke. His friend Max Brod testified: 'These jokes had to be childishly simple and must not be indecent.' (Indecent jokes were rejected by Kafka so resolutely that nobody would dare to tell them in his presence. It was simply impossible. He would smile politely and say: 'Disgusting!') Here's an example of a joke that would have had Kafka laughing:

'A millionaire, to whom a street beggar complains that he hasn't eaten for three days, answers kindly: 'One must try and force oneself!'

Czech society looks down on anybody who can't tell jokes well. Therefore uncommunicative individuals not only arm themselves with tear-gas spray against possible attackers when wandering about solo, but prudently memorise a fund of jokes in case they encounter a dubious character jumping out of a dark corner, grabbing them by the lapels and saying: 'Life is misery. Don't you know at least one good joke?'

In Japanese factories during the break the foreman leads his subordinates in physical exercise to loosen up their stiff bodies. In Czech offices and workshops it is quite normal for the boss to come among his subjects with something funny to tell. It's not enough just to laugh at the governor's joke, you need to be able to throw in one or two of your own.

"Czechs have a tradition of not taking things too seriously," said novelist Ivan Klíma. "Why? Maybe it's the philosophy of a nation that was never really free and always dominated by others. Cimrman is in this tradition. We've had a lot of famous Czechs in science and the arts, but Cimrman is our response not to get above ourselves."

> **Czech society looks down on anybody who can't tell jokes well.**

As an idiosyncratic and loveable wanderer who never quite achieves greatness, Cimrman is stitched into history's epoch-making moments by helping Marconi to discover radio, advising Johann Strauss on music, introducing Picasso to Cubism, and gaining notoriety for inventing the snowman. He conceives the idea that, if most wars are caused by big nations

35

wanting to get even bigger, then a Europe that consists of microscopic nations would be free from any strife.

Czechs consider their best authors to be humorists. A movie without sex could easily be a success, but without a hilarious catchphrase which the happy audience will endlessly repeat among their friends it wouldn't. Some of the most popular TV programmes are shows with candid cameras where the victim is firstly deceived, then demeaned and finally ostracised (in short, turned into a moron.) If someone on the screen falls down, it's a good reason for wild hilarity. The head of the family might taunt his wife, recalling a similar accident happening to her: "A pity I didn't have a video camera when you fell flat on your face with all the heavy shopping bags scattering around you!" And they will both laugh heartily. (Unless of course the wife still has her leg in plaster.)

> **"A movie without sex could easily be a success, but without a hilarious catchphrase it wouldn't."**

Czech humour know no bounds. Czechs are able to absorb dependency, slyness and even envy. One theory says that the Czechs are so witty that they will laugh at their own jaundice. But closer to the truth may be the claim that their envy is so deep, it even infiltrates their humour.

Attitudes & Values

Adapt or be adapted

The ability to put up with a situation, adjusting as needs must, has been elevated to an art form by the Czechs.

During the course of the Middle Ages they started off as obedient Catholics, then they were fiery Protestants,

> **The ability to put up with a situation, adjusting as needs must, has been elevated to an art form.**

and finally they ended up devoutly Catholic again, all solely dependent on who was in charge. They started the 20th century as noble democrats, had a spell of being dedicated communists, and wound up being democrats again. These metamorphoses didn't take generations of social evolution; many Czechs have lived through such changes in a single lifetime. But before you go wagging your finger at this apparent lack of conviction or principle, consider the butterfly: from caterpillar, through chrysalis to a beautiful winged creature, all in one lifetime. Some Czechs have yet another thing in common with a butterfly, no backbone.

Wealth and success

The Czechs believe that you will never become wealthy by putting more effort into your work, or by being smart or just plain lucky. You can become wealthy only by means of deception or to the detriment of someone else.

When someone is skilled at something, they tend to hide it. American companies were surprised during interviews when potential employees, who spoke a fluent second language or understood computers well, only let on that they knew a little about them. Given their history, it's not so much modesty as caution. The Czechs are imbued with the maxim: 'It's not good to stand taller than others in the row' (to which they might privately add, 'in case you get singled out for punishment'). This philosophy may be behind the dislike men and women have for being seen going about in smart clothes. Foreign employers have problems with the Czech attitude to dressing because their employees travel to work in jeans and shirts and change at work.

> **❝The Czechs believe that you can become wealthy only by means of deception or to the detriment of someone else.❞**

But all around them there is this new, glittering and loud world. Even our little, typical Czech, the faithful descendant of the good old soldier Švejk, gets on board and gets 'sophisticated'. Or at least he tries. His standard of living has rocketed and keeping up with the Joneses is his new favourite sport. Keeping up with, but not passing...

As if to make up for their reticence, most Czechs insist on the use of titles earned by academic prowess;

these are even exhibited in their IDs, in their driving licences, and on their doorbells. When being introduced or spoken about they love to be addressed by their titles. Nobody finds anything odd about this. A title becomes a part of the family name. And there is an unbelievably large number of titles*. If someone points out to you that he is an Engineer, he is not trying to invite you to attend a lecture on the problems of reinforced concrete tensions in dam construction, he is trying to tell you that you should address

66 When being introduced or spoken about they love to be addressed by their titles. 99

him as such. "My name is Engineer Novotný." So, when he is caught speeding and the police see his title in his driving licence and refer to it, he is so delighted that the fine becomes immaterial.

As a student at university you have to memorise the precise title of all teachers because it would be a big mistake to use a lesser one (for instance, saying Sir Senior Lecturer, or Sir Associate Professor instead of Sir Professor). On the other hand, using a more important title than the teacher actually has can also be insulting because the teacher might think you are making fun of the fact that he hasn't as yet achieved the higher one.

* But not noble ones. Noble titles were banned by law after the First World War. This is probably because the majority of Czech holders of them were of German origin.

Religion

Czechs consider themselves to be the most atheistic nation in Europe. In a pensive moment Jára Cimrman writes: "I am such a complete atheist that I'm afraid God will punish me." It seems that Czechs, among the most godless and sceptical peoples in Europe, prefer fiction to flesh and blood when pondering reality.

Officially the dominant religion in the country is Roman Catholic followed by the Protestant Evangelical Church, which is based on the ideas of Jan Hus who tried to reform the Catholic Church in the 15th century. He is a Czech national hero. People idolise him. A man who fought for his faith, he was burned at the stake in 1415 for failing to relinquish his beliefs. His motto, 'The truth wins', is written on the flag of the nation's president. Unfortunately most presidents haven't understood the message.

❝ More than 70% of Czechs say they don't believe in God. However, more than half believe in amulets and horoscopes. ❞

Czechs are undoubtedly the world's least religious nation. Not that there aren't any believers amongst them, but they are few and far between. Five minutes after the end of Mass in St. Vitus Cathedral, the most important Catholic Church in the country, the 31 people there will be replaced by more than 1000 tourists.

More than 70% of Czechs say they don't believe in God. However, more than half of them believe in amulets and horoscopes, and one in ten still believes, even after 40 years of communism, in 'the faith' (Karl Marx). So you can't really say that most Czechs believe in nothing. What is known is what Czechs don't believe in: 90% of them don't believe in any kind of afterlife – including many of those who declare themselves Catholics. This explains why funerals are very unimportant to many families.

The Czechs have the highest cremation rate in Europe (95% of people in Prague are cremated), and half the people in Prague don't even have a proper funeral. Very often the caskets containing the ashes are never picked up by relatives.

Systems

Education

The political and social change that followed the 'Velvet Revolution'* in 1989 has had a profound impact on all aspects of society. This includes the education system, which has, almost overnight, been dramatically liberated. Gone is the old Soviet style of

* A Revolution because it swiftly ended decades of communist occupation, and Velvet because, without a single shot being fired, it was quick, calm and as smooth as velvet. Hence the separation of the Czechs from the Slovaks is often referred to as 'the Velvet Divorce'.

cast iron discipline, the oppressive atmosphere in class rooms, the grey uniformity, the daily 'forced down the throat' ideology classes.

However, there is a problem with this in that, by and large, they were not replaced with anything of real value. The pupils interpreted the term 'freedom' as a free-for-all. Many teachers lost the will to care about this tendency, having a lot of personal and professional problems of their own: they have had to retrain and try to master completely new systems, new materials, new styles, etc. Teachers of Russian (previously a compulsory language taught in all schools) had to switch to English or German, with predictable results and consequences.

> **66 The change that followed the 'Velvet Revolution' has had a profound impact on all aspects of society. 99**

The previously enforced grey equality and red discipline among pupils was also gone. The attitude of the newly rich section of society is naturally reflected in their children and their behaviour in the class. The average pay of a typical teacher is low, to say the very least. Often the pocket money provided to many pupils by their parents exceeds the net monthly income of their teachers.

Transport

The public transport system in most Czech cities is good and a lot of people prefer it to going by car.

In Prague the most popular method (apart from the metro) is a tram. Some run all night long, so if you leave a party at 3 or 4 in the morning you don't have to call a taxi, you take a night tram. But try not to fall asleep: if you do, you're an easy target for pickpockets. Another hazard is the ticket inspectors. They get their thrills uncovering little mistakes, like your having stamped your ticket on the wrong side, and are not renowned for being affable. There are rumours that when they reach an impasse in their argument, they simply throw the ticket out of the window and say victoriously to the hapless passenger: "You don't have a ticket, so what are you telling me?"

Crossing the street is another danger. Beware not only cars, but trams. There is a law that on zebra crossings trams come first: most tram drivers assert this, but most tourists are ignorant of it, so while peacefully crossing a street they are rendered witless by a ringing tram monster suddenly charging up to them like a torpedo.

> **Beware not only cars, but trams. There is a law that on zebra crossings trams come first.**

The only Czech city with a metro system is Prague. It's much faster than trams or buses, but very deep and you spend a really long time travelling down the escalators. One of the reasons why it is so deep is because it was designed to double as a huge atomic shelter in case of conflict with the West. There are two sorts of escalators, the old Soviet ones and the new German type. The Soviet escalators are extremely fast and they can't be slowed down, so when an elderly person steps on them they get an adrenalin rush included in the price of the ticket.

As for the rest of the country, public transport is provided in the main by an anachronistic, dirty and dilapidated railway network (surviving from the time of the Austro-Hungarian Empire) which is rapidly losing out to a very efficient, modern and cheap coach transport system. Czech Railways are trying to fight back by introducing state-of-the-art, super-sensitive Italian trains, but most of them conk out on the antiquated tracks either as soon as they leave the station or somewhere in the middle of a potato field.

> **❝The railway lines will no doubt improve, but the modern high speed trains will probably be 50-year-old dirties by then. ❞**

The railway lines will no doubt improve, but the modern high speed trains will probably be 50-year-old dirties by then.

Crime and punishment

The crime rate in the country is lower than the E.U. average, but Czechia has, in fact, as large a prison population as any other. This has less to do with shoplifting (which is so prevalent that in the supermarket the basket/trolley rule is generally strictly enforced so that even if you explain that all you want is a carton of milk, the staff often insist on your using a basket or trolley anyway).

It is more likely because Parliament produces a lot of misleading and confusing laws. For instance, one law says that you don't have to report a close family member who breaks the law, and another law says that for traffic offences the driver of the vehicle is responsible, not the owner. So you do what clever Czechs do. You park your car incorrectly and you get a ticket. You go to the police station and there you say that it wasn't you who parked the car, it was a close member of the family. And because by right you don't have to reveal his or her name, the police have to let you off.

> **A trip to a police station shows that not much has changed... the furniture and atmosphere of the communist era linger on.**

It has been said that the Czech police are: as sour as an Austrian, as strict as a German, as lazy as a Greek, as corrupt as an Italian, and as chaotic as a Turk. An iffy combination. A trip to a police station shows that not much has changed in the last two decades: the uniforms may be different but the furniture and atmosphere of the communist era linger on. At many stations, the good old rickety-rackety typewriters are still in use. The force is gradually being equipped with PCs, but rumour has it that most policemen don't even know how to switch one on.

Behaviour

The family today

During communism there were no private businesses in the country, and instead of building financial security many people built homes and families as a method of inner escape. Thus, despite an increasing number of singles and co-habitees in society, most Czechs still live in a nuclear family with the man at the head of it, or so he pretends in public.

> 66 **Most Czechs still live in a nuclear family with the man at the head of it, or so he pretends.** 99

Before communism the man would go to work to earn money and the wife would stay at home and take care of the family and home. During communism almost all women were made to work and men would still expect them to take care of the family and home. These days the woman works by choice, and the man comes home, tells his wife that there is no beer in the fridge, asks her "What are we having for dinner?" and then goes to watch TV.

The privatisation that took place at the end of communism was a male dominated privatisation and men had it all their own way. Men make on average about 30% more money than women even when working in the same job and position. They are also in the majority in government and parliament.

Discrimination against women is well documented

in Czech legend. In the story of Queen Libuše, the men complain that they don't want to have a woman as head of the country anymore. When the Queen asks why, she is told that 'Women's hair may be long, but their brains are short', and they know what they are talking about because they are 'already ruled by them – at home'.

The elderly

The only advantage of being old in Czechia is that younger people offer you a seat in a bus or a tram. This can also happen to you if you're male – even a comparatively young one. The travelling public find it quite natural if a man in his 50s is happily ogling a sexy teenage girl and she stands up and offers him her seat.

Other than this, being a senior citizen in Czechia is hard work. They have to live on a very small pension and their standard of life is really **66 Being a senior citizen in Czechia is hard work... It's no wonder many still vote for the Communist party. 99** very basic. During communism they did not have the opportunity to save money, so now they have to suffer while all around them they see people taking advantage of the new prosperity that capitalism has to offer. It's no wonder that many of the elderly still vote for the Communist party.

How the Czechs behave towards their children

Much like the rest of Europe, the Czech Republic has a negative birthrate. The average Czech woman will give birth to 1.3 children in her lifetime. This, naturally, is not even enough to maintain the current population.

The few Czech children that are born are forever mummy's little darlings. Indeed, in the eyes of his or her parents, a Czech remains a child regardless of how old he or she is. A Czech child will be supported financially by his parents until well into his fifties. In return, the parents have complete control over his life. This lack of independence is fostered by the school system, which essentially requires the child to absorb huge amounts of largely irrelevant information without requiring any real understanding of it. After several gruelling years of schooling the child comes full circle: he still knows absolutely nothing.

66 A Czech child will be supported by his parents until well into his fifties. In return, the parents have complete control over his life. 99

What this system of education will have achieved, however, is to replace simple childish ignorance with a fully qualified sense of confusion about the world. The child is thus totally unequipped to deal with life, which fulfils the aim of rearing generation after generation of fully dependent offspring.

How the Czechs behave towards their parents

All Czech children (young and old) regard their parents as their greatest enemies, the enemies of the entire universe even. They wonder to themselves: "How could someone as intelligent and witty as I am be born to such complete imbeciles?" The conclusion they invariably reach is that there must have been some terrible mistake at the hospital and they were swapped at birth. Children growing up in the Czech Republic today will in future be regarded not so much as the 'lost generation' but as the 'swapped generation'.

In spite of this, Czechs continue to borrow money from their (clearly not biological) parents, which as a matter of principle is never repaid, and on top of this they expect to inherit their non-parents' house as soon as they pack their bags and shuffle off to the country cottage for good.

Outsiders now have sufficient understanding of Czech inter-generational relationships to be able to answer the following question: "Where do elderly people in the Czech Republic spend their twilight years?"

a. in the family home surrounded by loving children and adoring grandchildren;

b. in the old people's home in a shared room;

c. alone in a small, damp, cold room waiting for the phone to ring.

Answer: This is a trick question. Czech parents aren't daft enough to bother waiting by the phone; they know it won't ever ring.

How the Czechs behave towards animals

If it was possible to do so, the average Czech would rather offer his seat on the tram to his dog, cat or parrot than to an elderly person. Dogs are allowed in restaurants and cafés, and in many cases the establishment automatically provides them with a bowl of water. Pets, unlike the elderly, are regarded as full members of the family. This contrasts with the Czech attitude to farm animals who, once they've ceased to be useful, almost always end up served with dumplings in goulash.

How the Czechs behave towards minorities

It is an unfortunate fact that Czechs generally treat ethnic minorities worse than they do farm animals. Ask a Czech person to explain this and he'll say that horses are better at pulling carts and cows taste better.

Czech behaviour behind the steering wheel

The Czech Republic is a small country; if you put your mind to it, you can drive from north to south across the country in two hours and from east to west in four. A journey of 50km (31 miles) is regarded therefore as a long haul which warrants a great deal of preparation. This means that the Czechs do not have any real concept of a true long distance journey (apart perhaps from au pairs, who regularly take the coach from Prague to London).

Czech drivers refuse to take breaks from driving and they combat fatigue by long mobile phone conversations with their mates at their destination. The phone is, incidentally, held in the left hand, a cigarette in the right, which means steering is done by the forearms and changing gears is done by the knees.

> **...steering is done by the forearms and changing gears is done by the knees.**

A sort of Czech national sport is to enjoy a trip by car without having a driving licence. In one six-month period in 2006 the police caught more than 8,000 drivers who didn't have one. A newspaper even reported one instance of a 'professional' driver who had only a licence for a moped and who was caught repeatedly by police while driving a bus full of people. His excuse was that he wanted to help out while there was a serious shortage of bus drivers.

An average Czech driver does 10,000 km a year, which is the lowest average in the E.U. The reason for the low mileage is probably related to typical Czech indolence. When your job is more than a few miles from your home then it is too far: Czechs prefer to work just a few minutes by bus from their house. Then, in the summer, thousands of drivers get into their car and drive 2,000 kilometres in one day to the Croatian coast and, surprise, surprise, crash their car there. Plenty of Czech drivers die every summer in Croatia, and Croatians are always scared to death when they see a car bearing the letters 'CZ'.

Conversation & Gestures

Everything is controversial

You can talk with a Czech about anything, but tread warily. With political or sporting subjects it is prudent to establish first, by means of diplomatically innocent questions, the leanings of the others and pretend that you share them. Sometimes even such an innocent subject as the weather could be a controversial issue. A typical Czech is always prepared to argue, loudly and without restraint, over just about anything. The less he actually understands the matter, the better. In discussions then, the winner is not the one who used the best arguments, but the one who talked and shouted the most.

> **A typical Czech is always prepared to argue, loudly and without restraint, over just about anything.**

Insults

There are languages in which people insult each other by using flowery sentences, where it takes time, will and word-power to insult someone. The Czechs have it much simpler: their language offers hundreds of one or two-word insults. In an American movie about adolescents one particular term that was frequently used was 'Shit!' In the Czech dubbing of the film, this term was translated into 27 different equivalents.

The Czechs have a store of different insults for their acquaintances and for total strangers. They have insults which denote affection and tenderness, and others that are downright excoriating. You can insult anyone very simply by likening him to an animal. Any animal*. The only exception so far is a butcher bird and a fruit bat – two creatures that have not, as yet, featured in any Czech swearword or insult.

One Czech insult is embodied in a graphic symbol and used worldwide. Drawn on walls from a Prague public toilet to a Fifth Avenue sidewalk, it depicts a basic part of the female anatomy. It also signals to a Czech that another Czech has been there.

By curious coincidence, it is identical to the sign on the 'start' button of almost every photocopier. When this equipment started to be available in the Czech

---

* But for no known reason, an ox is the worst.

Republic following the fall of communism, it caused great national amusement to see the symbol used like this.

The Czechs harbour in their behaviour a quaint contradiction – mutual affection can be expressed by juicy insults. To proclaim that you respect and revere someone – or even that you actually like him – is socially totally unacceptable. You will discredit not only him, but yourself as well. Thus, to question anyone's intelligence is fairly safe, and you can use idiot, imbecile, cretin, moron, prick, with happy abandon. However, to say in a quiet and collected tone something like, "It seems to me you're being really silly" would be to invite trouble. No Czech will passively stand such an insult.

> **66 The Czechs harbour a quaint contradiction – mutual affection can be expressed by juicy insults. 99**

Gestures and greetings

By and large the Czechs do not gesticulate. When greeting a woman, a man may sometimes try to peck her on the cheek but they would rather shake hands. If someone grabs your hand and squeezes it painfully, it just means the person is pleased to see you. The harder the squeeze and the longer the shake, the more affectionate it is.

A handshake signals a certain formality: the best

and closest friends never shake hands. They usually mumble some sort of greeting and if they still feel that physical contact is desirable, then it's a hard but friendly smack on the shoulder or a kick to the ankle. The signal they emit to the world is that they are so close they can afford to greet each other in such a manner.

The degree of inter-personal proximity is also expressed by using either the formal surname style when addressing someone, or the more matey first name manner. The latter is strictly reserved for close pals. You have to be acquainted for some considerable time and then still have to be invited to change to the informal form.

The formal greeting is "Dobrý den" ("Good day"). The informal greeting is "Ahoy!" If you think that most Czechs are seamen,

> **66 Never hug someone in public, especially if you are of the same gender. 99**

you'd be wrong. Czechs live in a hopelessly landlocked country. This nautical expression was universally adopted as an informal greeting as long ago as the end of the First World War, and nobody knows how or why. One theory is that Czechs are thus rather romantically compensating for the absence of the sea.

Finally, a word of warning: never, under any circumstances, hug someone in public, especially if you are of the same gender. The Czechs are not prepared for it and may pick up confusing sexual signals.

55

Embraces are strictly reserved for occasions like funerals and the gravest life or death situations.

Beer

'Hunger is just a masked thirst', is a popular bon mot among the regulars in Czech pubs and the thirst quencher they have in mind is beer. But beer is not just a lubricant, not by a long chalk. It's a source of national pride – the fluid, fundamental essence of being Czech.

When you want to start a conversation with a Czech and you are not sure about what to talk about, then talking about beer is an ideal opener. Just remember that you can criticise almost everything, but not Czech beer. If you wish to discredit yourself forever in society, just remark that quite good beer is also to be found, for example, in Belgium. Every Czech orthodox beer drinker knows that everywhere else in the world people produce and consume only undrinkable swill, and that even such famous brands as Heineken don't measure up to the smallest regional Czech brewery. It is wise to remember that you are in a country where a former prime minister on an official visit to a neighbouring state publicly proclaimed its beer to be

> **Czech beer is not just a lubricant. It's a source of national pride.**

only good "for cleansing dentures".

One of the best ice hockey full-backs in the history of the game Jan Suchý did not fill his water bottle with some sort of isotonic drink for his training sessions like his team-mates did, but good old Czech beer. Before matches he would knock back a regular shot or two so he didn't have to strain himself with warm-up exercises.

In the hearts of its consumers Czech beer stands only one comparison: that of Irish beer. But you have to add that Irish beers have an entirely different character, sugar content and who knows what else, and therefore in all fairness, with Czech "capped" (as they affectionately dub its huge foam head) beer it simply cannot be compared at all.

> **Czechs are not only good at brewing beer, they are exceptionally good at drinking it.**

There are many different types of beer called Pils or Pilsner around the world, but only one that is authentic and brewed in the city of Pilsen and that is Pilsner Urquell. Pilsen is considered by Czechs to be the world's capital of beer, which is closely followed by beer from Budweiser-Budvar. Never confuse the American Budweiser with the Czech beer of the same name. There is currently a court battle over who is allowed to use the trademark Budweiser. The Czechs don't quite understand all this palaver since they were brewing beer in the city of Budweiss long before

America was even discovered. Back then it was not necessary to register trademarks.

Czechs are not only good at brewing beer, they are exceptionally good at drinking it. Czechia has the highest consumption of beer per person in the world. They successfully defend this sovereign position year after year even though the score is being spoiled a little by the Moravians (Czechs living in the eastern half of the state) who somewhat perversely prefer wine. Anyway, to say about someone that he drinks like a fish (or as the locals say, "like a rainbow") is not a reproach, but a compliment.

“ You shouldn't be surprised if you run into a beer kiosk while walking in the deepest forest. ”

Apart from some banks, post offices and toy shops, you can buy beer almost everywhere, which means you will encounter a pub wherever you go. You shouldn't be surprised if you run into a beer kiosk while walking in the deepest forest. Well, there are some villages out in the sticks where they simply have no pub, but this is pointed out as a local peculiarity in tourist guides.

The culture of beer drinking – to which belong smoky pubs, unpolished pumps and thick glass beer mugs with a handle – has been praised by many Czech writers. Jaroslav Hašek (author of *Soldier Švejk*) and Bohumil Hrabal (author of the book on which the (1965) Oscar winning film *Closely Observed Trains* was based)

58

created their masterpieces in pubs of this sort.

Czech scholars and intellectuals do from time to time step into the ring to hit out against alcoholism. Last time this happened was during the so-called 'national awakening' in the mid-19th century. When the then national leader, Josef Jungmann (his German surname was no hindrance to his patriotism), informed the public about the start of a prohibition campaign, he added immediately and expressly that this obviously did not refer to beer drinking. Even during the communist domination, the small talk in pubs prophesied that a government that raised the price of beer would fall.

> **Even during communist domination, the small talk in pubs prophesied that a government that raised the price of beer would fall.**

In many folk songs the exalted virtue of beer drinking is merged with the ancient national struggle: 'When the Czechs have a drink of beer – they'll fight like lions without fear' goes one ditty about a one-time fight against the Germans. It suggests that the Germans did not drink (or did, but much less) and were therefore defeated.

In a serious poll which posed the question 'What are the Czechs better at than all other nations?' a quarter of respondents answered 'beer drinking'. Small wonder: we are talking about a country where ex-president Havel took his counterpart Clinton, not to visit the gothic relics of Prague, but to a pub.

Becherovka

Another national drink is the apéritif Becherovka, a dazzling yellow spirit in a green bottle made with 20 herbs. It was originally invented as a medicine for the stomach and is therefore, despite being 38% proof, acceptable as a small dose before lunch, even for teetotallers.

❝ Czech dishes are delicious, heavy, and atrociously unhealthy. ❞

Don't ask what it tastes like. It tastes just like Becherovka, and nothing else in the world tastes like it. Only three people in the whole world know how to make it and they are never allowed to travel together in the same car or plane in case they have an accident and the recipe is lost forever.

Food

Czech dishes are delicious, heavy. and atrociously unhealthy. They are based on an unbelievable amount of (if possible mainly animal) fat. The more of it, the more the dish is ethnically Czech, and therefore that much better. A good soup must have specks of fat floating on it and the meat of the main dish must swim in rendered-down fat.

A key item is dumplings – slices of leavened dough

boiled in water – which make a great sponge for the sauces that accompany, for example, Goulash or Svíčková. Czech Goulash has nothing in common with the original Hungarian Goulash. It's pork or beef stew thickened with flour and usually eaten with dumplings, or boiled potatoes or bread. Pork with cabbage and dumplings is widely held to be the national dish, but most Czechs would place Svíčková in pole position – beef with dumplings, cream sauce and cranberries. Dumplings, together with a rich sauce, fatty meat and cabbage, represent not only the favourite ethnic dish, but also a true calorie/cholesterol bombshell.

> **The Czechs will even fry cheese and serve it with a dollop of tartar sauce on top.**

Eating in Czechia is a vegetarian's nightmare. What the Czechs understand by the term vegetarian is fried vegetables. They will fry cauliflower for you, or mushrooms or eggplant. They will even fry cheese and serve it with a dollop of tartar sauce on top.

The second most popular national dish – which also happens to be the traditional Christmas dish – is carp. There are hundreds of recipes on how to prepare it, but it is mainly served crumbed and fried. If ever you are in the Czech Republic over the Christmas period you will find tubs full of living carp in every Czech town. People buy one, bring it home, leave it for a day or so in the bath (during which time

no-one can take a shower) and the kids play with it.
The carp has to suffer this until the day when the
father of the household kills it, usually with a meat

> **66 Occasionally the family gets so attached to the carp that they give it a name. 99**

mallet. Then it is cooked and
served with homemade potato
salad.

Occasionally the family gets so
attached to the carp in their
bathtub that they give it a name, and then instead of
eating it they throw it into the river where, because of
the change in temperature, the carp dies of shock.

If you're a bit peckish

To complement Czech beer there are some special
snacks, for instance, brawn with onion, black pepper
and vinegar, or pickled cheese, or pickled sausage, or
the Czech speciality, beer cheese. Should you ask in a
pub for some beer cheese you will receive a piece of
really stinky cheese together with sliced onion and
mustard.

After you've got it, you face the problem of how to
eat it. Take your fork and mash it all together (3 minutes). Then make a hollow in the middle of it, pour a
splash of beer into it, mix it (30 seconds) and spread a
thick layer of it on a slice of bread.

Don't even think about this dish if planning to go
on a date the same day.

Health

The standard of healthcare in the Czech Republic is relatively high. The problem is that people are used to getting everything free of charge, and since the year 2000 they have had to pay for some minor items. They dislike this and reminisce about the 'great' communist days – free minor items. Hospital patients pay nothing for medical care or for accommodation and food yet they complain that the food is poor and they would have better food at home, forgetting that at home they would have to buy it.

All surgery and operations are free, but you may have to wait a year or two. If you want to shorten the waiting time you can try to slip the doctor an incentive. When you ask Czech doctors if something like this is going on, they all say "I've heard of it, but it doesn't happen here." Every Czech knows that you should give your doctor a bottle of something. Doctors are either all alcoholics, or they are in the spirit-selling business.

> **Operations are free, but you may have to wait a year or two. If you want to shorten the waiting time you can try to slip the doctor an incentive.**

Research has revealed that Czech doctors do not know how to communicate with their patients. As they are not trained in communication, patient individuality is irrelevant to them and a typical comment might be: "I mean Mr. Gall Bladder in room 5."

For doctors the organ is always more important than the patient.

A specifically Czech disease is intestinal cancer: the Czechs lead Europe in this. The reason, it seems, is lots of beer. Some years ago billboards were put up all over the country showing a line-up of patients with the disease. The picture was similar to that of the Czech ice-hockey team which declared: "We are the champions!"

Leisure & Fun

Just as 'Hoover' is a synonym for vacuum cleaner, Croatia is for most Czechs synonymous with a summer holiday. What attracts them there is the breathtaking coastline and the fact that the local language, being a Slavic tongue, is fairly easy to under-stand. Less attractive to them however are the sea urchins and the local prices – for every Czech is basically a penny pincher.

66 Every Czech is basically a penny pincher. 99

It's a trait that best shows itself in the summer time. A lot of Croatian hotel and restaurant keepers could tell you a tale or two about this. A typical Czech holidaymaker carries with him in a suitcase from home, where the prices are a lot cheaper, piles of tinned food, rolls of salami, packets of soup, etc. To go to a restaurant to eat or drink while abroad is for an average Czech as much a sin as it would be to leave his car in a paid parking space when there is a free place only a few miles away.

A good few times in the past the population's savings were lost either by war or by fraud so their forefathers saved in small local co-operatives, and their descendants carry on the custom today. Our little Czech will not, however, invest his savings in entrance fees for museums, nor will he spend them in casinos or on donations to Save the Dolphin charities. Neither will he buy himself some valuable souvenir. No sir! He will bring home something much more whole-some, much more practical – like curtains.

> **66** Most often, he will do with his money the best possible thing there is to do – he will save it. **99**

But most often, after comparing the prices with prices at home, he will quickly put his wallet back in his pocket. And later he will do with his money the best possible thing there is to do – he will save it. Small wonder, then, that a Croatian shop-keeper would rather a bag lady stepped into his shop than a Czech.

Prize competitions

To make Big Money by honest toil is impossible – our Czech tried that last Tuesday and… nothing! To steal

Big Money is somewhat immoral, but mainly it's dangerous. To inherit a fortune does not bring the right thrill, only the taxman and other relatives. The only satisfactory way to make a healthy bundle is to win it.

To go to a casino is not an option; he is not quite sure what to do there and anyway he nurses the suspicion that it's not all that transparent and above board. So, if you discount medieval treasure hunting, the only avenue left is the lottery. The risk is manageable, prizes adequate, and the danger of losing all one's winnings to a call girl at the bar is minimal.

❝One of the cardinal sins which can never be forgiven is success and riches. ❞

There are many lotteries, weekly draws and pools and they are all mightily popular. However, the prospect of winning a really huge fortune has a slightly schizophrenic impact on the Czech gambler. He is actually afraid of it. The Czechs being a truly egalitarian nation are perfectly aware that one of the cardinal sins which can never be forgiven, not even by one's closest friends, is success and riches. So, he only plays modestly. And the unspent money he takes away – and saves.

Pubbing

From work to the pub and then home. Pubs close relatively late and beer is not much more expensive there than in the supermarkets.

The pub is a place where problems are solved. It is not a place where you talk about your accomplishments, but a place where you can let go of your frustrations for a while. You talk about how stupid the government is, you criticise your boss and your wife and you discuss sports.

Weekend shopping

At the weekends, when not in the country, a husband doesn't go to a pub that often because he has to drive his wife to a shopping centre. During the 40+ years of communism there were no opportunities to shop for Western goods, but illegally sold Western magazines gave people insights into Western fashions, electronics and cars. These days the lure of consumerism beckons, so on Sundays instead of going to church, people spend hours in the new temples to prosperity.

Sex? Shush!

The Czechs are a nation of prudes, though they are not fully aware of this. The typical male speaks about sex only with his closest friends. Among them he likes to boast and sound worldly. Many, however, still don't quite understand that sex is not a 100 metre sprint and the winner is not the one who crosses the finish line first.

Apart from this, sex issues are not usually mentioned much. That includes even parents and their off-spring, the parental reasoning being that they are still far too young for it. This strategy frequently lasts until the moment when their 15-year-old daughter comes home pregnant. The sex issue is like the proverbial iceberg, with most of it hidden deep under water.

> **66 Come spring and every navigable river is besieged by Czechs 'doing the river'. 99**

Canoeing

Canoeing is for some Czechs a sport, for others a trip or a party or a way to entertain the kids. Come spring and with the first sunny weekend the madness starts: every navigable river is besieged by Czechs 'doing the river', from a professional in the appropriate dress for hard training, to a raft made of planks and tyres carrying a keg of beer and friends with the bellies to match. Olympic medallist Lukáš Pollert, a canoeing and kayaking legend, recommends beer as the best of ion drinks.

On soft summer nights along the banks you will encounter picturesque tented camps with campfires and the romantic sound of guitar strings. In late autumn people pack up their canoes and boats to await the longed-for 'opening of the river', a carnival of the funniest or most ridiculous boats, floats, rafts or crafts of any kind which starts the season the following spring.

The law of river demands that canoeists salute each other with "Ahoy!". A Czech crossing a bridge or walking beside the river will also shout "Ahoy!" to passing canoes, and canoeists will shout back in unison "Ahooooy!"

Other sports – especially a passive one

The Czechs know they are the best ice-hockey players in the world (for example: Jaromír Jágr), and only a born-and-bred Canadian with a Vancouver Canucks season ticket in his pocket could possibly disagree. After the Czech team won Olympic gold in Nagano, Japan, the Czech people demanded that the captain of the national team become President. An opera was specially composed about this huge triumph and performed in the National Theatre.

> **❝Every Czech knows that he is a member of a nation of champions – and therefore he himself is also a champion, in a way...❞**

The Czechs are also the best soccer players (for example, Pavel Nedvěd), the best athletes (Roman Dvořák), phenomenal tennis players (Martina Navrátilová), and so on. So, every Czech knows that he is a member of a nation of champions – and therefore he himself is also a champion, in a way...

Whenever there is any kind of international championship in progress, the Czech fan will join thousands of other similarly excited fans in front of a giant TV screen on the main square of the historic centre of Prague as well as in most other large towns, and will jeer, scream and get intoxicated. Also, along with all the others, he will rhythmically hop up and down on the spot while shouting "Whoever isn't jumping isn't a Czech!" and will probably try to make the passing group of bewildered Japanese tourists do the same. But God forbid that the Czech team loses. The jumping will still go on, only the previously happy drunks will turn ugly. Should this happen, the best advice for any visitors in the vicinity is to quietly disappear.

66 The Czechs have cunningly invented a number of specific sports which are played only by them and nowhere else in the world. 99

In order to pre-empt this and avoid instances of the home teams losing, the Czechs have cunningly invented a number of specific sport disciplines which are played only by them and nowhere else in the world. They are, therefore, the unchallenged world champions of these games – games like cycle-ball, Czech hand-ball (with a different size of playing field and different rules), leg-ball (a summer alternative to beach volleyball but played with one's legs).

There are so many disciplines in which the Czechs

are dominant that the average individual only has time to be a spectator, and does not attempt any sport whatsoever. This means he has just enough time to sit long into the night in front of the TV watching the sport channel, equipped with an adequate supply of beer and crisps; he even opens the window now and then to let the fresh air in.

Business

First the good news

If Ivana Trump is omitted as an example, the most famous Czech business person would be Tom Baťa. Mr. Baťa was a cobbler from a poor Moravian village who expanded to the whole world in the 1930s, despite the world-wide recession at the time. His firm still exists around the globe to this day

Then the bad

Czech people love their freedom. But the freedom has always been limited to their private sphere. Work is seen as an unpleasant and inevitable part of life – it just has to be endured.

Productivity in most Czech firms is not dazzlingly high. To tell the truth, it's very often nearly zero;

almost as if the Czechs are trying to fulfil the words of the anonymous classic: 'I love work and labour – I can easily watch them for hours.'

The earnings in some companies are well below average and yet there is still a fair amount of demand to work there.

The secret is that besides the actual pay, there is a bonus: the chance to pilfer. The employer pays his people a bit less, but he turns a blind eye if they filch something from the production line now and then. Everybody knows that everybody is involved and therefore nobody can spill the beans. The workforce thus improves their remuneration and enjoys a warm feeling knowing that they have outfoxed the boss. The boss, of course, knows all about it and he uses this to keep his employees in line. Should they ever demand a rise, he will threaten them with a tighter regime and restricted chance to steal.

> **66 The secret is that besides the actual pay, there is a bonus: the chance to pilfer. 99**

This phenomenon of industrial peace based on a symbiosis of enterprise and criminality is something that lives on from the old communist times. It's a wonder no-one has made a proper study of this and got a Nobel Prize for it; maybe not the Economics prize, but perhaps the Peace one – for eternal social harmony.

Customs & Traditions

From one anniversary to the next

The Czechs like to celebrate. Or perhaps one should say the Czech men like to celebrate: all the time and everywhere. In the office, in the pubs, in the open, the venue is unimportant, and very often so is the reason. What really counts is the frequency. As often as possible is the desired norm.

Some say the roots of this unquenchable quest for debauchery and intoxicated fun evolved during the communist era when the workers felt they needed to amuse themselves at work somehow. However, traces of this attitude prevail to this day, much to the alarm and sorrow of the nation's economists and managers.

❝ The Czechs like to celebrate. Or perhaps one should say the Czech men like to celebrate: all the time and everywhere. ❞

The Czechs can always find a good excuse to be merry. As well as the universally accepted birthdays, they also celebrate so-called name days, when a particular Christian name is allocated to a particular date – and many people place more importance on name days than on birthdays. On a name day, the honoured person does not expect any real or expensive presents. A bottle or two (or more) – which will be consumed almost immediately on the spot – will do nicely. Often the celebrations will carry on after working hours and spill into a nearby pub. The most popular name days like Joseph, Frantisek or Jan could easily rival the wild and carefree abandon of a New Year's Eve bash. The ladies celebrate their name days only very rarely: instead they have their men to celebrate them for them. So one sees massive masculine outbursts of jollity on popular feminine name days like Marie or Anne – without many females in sight.

What perhaps takes the biscuit in this male/female celebratory imbalance is International Women's Day (8th March). A number of offices and factories actually cease to perform on that day. The workforce usually gathers in the company communal hall and the honoured females – having first prepared platters of snacks to accompany the employer's contribution in the form of booze – wait on the males who graciously do the demanding job that this celebration requires of them. And so it goes merrily around, year after year.

Music

Czechs say that inside every Czech there is a musician. The saying goes back to the 18th and 19th centuries when Czech musicians were employed all over Europe. It is certainly an exaggeration, but it is a fact that Czechia has many People's Music Schools, where youngsters get educated in classical music and learn to play one or two instruments.

A few famous composers were born in the country in the 19th century and Czechs are very proud of them. Prague in particular is a city of music with as many as 15 classical music concerts taking place daily.

In order to have a decent conversation with the Czechs it is a good idea to know some basics about Czech classical composers and their works. Bedřich Smetana was the founder of Czech classical music. His most famous work is the symphonic poem 'My Country' which comprises six parts, each of which describes a beautiful place in Czechia. The best known part is the second which describes the river Vltava (Moldau) flowing from its source through the Czech countryside, on to Prague and eventually into the river Elbe.

66 Dvořák's Symphony No.9 from the New World was the first music ever broadcast from the Moon. 99

Another famous composer was Antonín Dvořák, an impoverished butcher, who became the first director of the National Conservatory in New York, and whose music was the first to sound 'heavenly'. His Symphony No.9 from the New World was the first music ever broadcast from the Moon. Apollo 11 took a recording there and played it to the whole world after landing.

In the 19th century Czechs embraced their folk music. National tunes spread from the countryside to the towns. One popular Czech song that became world famous was a polka composed by a certain Mr. Vejvoda. It became *Roll Out The Barrel*.

Dancing class

Czech dance schools have a long tradition: they are social relics from the times of the Habsburg Monarchy. Boys and girls in the last year of high school are encouraged to attend dance class, where they learn not only classics like the waltz and the polka (a traditional Czech dance), but tango, cha-cha, salsa and contemporary dance too. Girls are usually in the majority as it is not that popular among boys, which is a shame, because dance classes are a great place to pick up a girl.

Most of the schools offer boys hefty discounts and some accept girls only if they come with a boy (not necessarily 'the boyfriend'). Many boys go to these schools, paid by their parents, simply because they have to. Some go because they are great places to fool around, such as throwing dozens of little balls onto the dance floor to make couples fall over. However, misbehaviour can lead to expulsion. One minor offence means that one corner of your registration card is cut off. If the third corner is cut then you have to leave the course. This means you can join those who do a regular bunk and spend a riotous time with your mates in a nearby pub instead.

Government & Bureaucracy

It is usual in Europe that people in cities vote more to the left and people in the countryside vote more to the right. Not in Czechia. Believe it: most workers in big factories vote for the right. Since the Velvet Revolution, Prague's officials have all been right wingers. The other paradox is that a typical right wing voter is young.

In the elections a party has to get more than 5% of the votes to enter the Lower Parliamentary Chamber, and usually five parties manage

> **❝ It was the first Czechoslovak President, Masaryk, who said: 'Every nation gets the government it deserves.' ❞**

this. One of them is always the Communist Party. There is an unwritten law that none of the other parties can make a government coalition with them. However, after the 2007 elections neither the left nor the right had a majority without them. Talk concerning the composition of the government went on for more than six months and the country was for all practical purposes governmentless. And, surprise surprise, things went from strength to strength.

Many people loved this period of 'non-governmental interference'. But Czechs have always been very sceptical about their governments. It was the first Czechoslovak President, Masaryk, who said: "Every nation gets the government it deserves." In

Czechia, every Czech is a pub expert on how to govern the country and every Czech knows how to build a stable, strong and prosperous state. Naturally, the level of simultaneous beer consumption greatly influences the quality and depth of these suggestions. Unfortunately – or fortunately – this is often lost on the politicians of the day.

The head of state is The President. The position is ceremonial – he doesn't have too much power, but for Czechs the President is an important icon. With the exception of the first and last Presidents of Czechoslovakia and the Czech Republic, it seems that to become President it is necessary to spend some time in prison: 9 out of 11 former Presidents had a spell in jail. President Masaryk was never imprisoned but was sentenced to death in his absence.

> **Every Czech is an expert on how to govern the country and every Czech knows how to build a stable and strong and prosperous state.**

Maybe it bodes well that the last Czech President was neither imprisoned nor given a death sentence. There may no longer be a need to elect only heroes and rebels as Presidents. Boring economists could qualify too.

Members of Parliament have a cushy life: state benefits – the good life; salary – low taxation (i.e. nothing); personal assistants – employing their nearest and dearest to make more money (thus keeping it in the family); free passes on public transport.

They also have exclusive use of the special Parliamentary restaurant, where the prices are three times lower than in the cheapest pub in the city. An added perk is being allowed to drink alcohol during parliamentary sessions. This, plus the token price, means that all too often many are not able to produce a coherent thought, let alone cast a vote on one.

Dealing with civil servants

Because Czech people tend to resolve their private matters during working hours, the whole working day is organised to gain as much time as possible to devote to them. This means that as a customer you have to know how a Czech civil servant ticks. It is, for example, not a good idea to enter a municipal or State office with a request on a Monday or a Friday. On Mondays, everyone is busy talking about the weekend just passed. Fridays, in turn, are used to plan and organise the weekend to come. Even the remaining days are not really convenient. During these days, the civil servant has to go and see his GP, his financial adviser, etc. So one can understand that civil servants are always grumpy and hardly ever make an effort to meet one's needs.

> **The whole working day is organised to gain as much time as possible to devote to private matters.**

79

So Czech people have had to find a way round this problem. The majority of permissions or stamps for a project, say, to build a house, are not needed anyway, because the project has been started without any. A fine is, after all, easier to bear than the hassle caused by trying to get all the permissions from the different departments.

Knowing the rules means knowing how to bypass them. Czechs are very aware that the State institutions are slow to check whether someone has complied with the proper procedures. By the time they eventually get their act together and check up on you, the laws will already have changed. They keep changing because the government loves playing musical chairs – the only thing that Czech politicians are really good at.

> **66 Knowing the rules means knowing how to bypass them. By the time they check up on you, the laws will already have changed. 99**

In cases where the civil servants still insist on making your life difficult you go for the alternative solution. In the Czech Republic the family is more powerful than the State. In practice this means that you just open your address book in which every name carries a note stating where this person is working and how this could be useful to you. You will nearly always find someone in the right position to help you. To deal with this, you can easily spend all your working hours.

Language & Ideas

The Czech language is a very old and a very intensely scientifically-honed tongue. Its alphabet has 42 letters, and foreigners, with tongue firmly in cheek, often compare it with Chinese. Since most of the time in its historic past the Czech lands were under German rule, the language only survived through use by peasants in remote villages. It was only towards the end of the 19th century that some enlightened patriots started to resurrect it and tried to give it order, style, vocabulary and system. Many words had to be artificially created, grammar invented and pronunciation established. The end product is the result of decades of hard work by a small army of patriotic scientists, professors, poets and writers.

As one would expect from these classic intellectuals, the language thus created is so complicated and involved that it takes a lifetime to learn it

> **The language is so complicated that it takes a lifetime to learn it properly, even for many born-and-bred Czechs.**

properly, even for many born-and-bred Czechs. Among many other traps, it has for example seven grammatical cases (compare: English has one, German and Greek both have four). Hungarian and Finnish may be even more complicated, but the Czechs would concur with the suggestion that the classic reference to Greek lingo is insufficiently adequate: it should have been changed a long time ago to "It's all Czech to me!"

Sex in Czech

Czech surnames have male and female versions. The female is derived from the male usually with the addition of an '-á' or '-ová'. This means that in Czech newspapers you will read about Madeleine Albrightová or Madonová. Few Czechs know that Chanel was female because the French neglected to add the ending '-ová' to the Chanel perfume boxes that were sold in Czechia.

"Czech surnames have male and female versions."

In most European languages the word 'man' has two meanings: male human and mankind, a fact that makes feminists moan. The Czech language distinguishes between '*muz*' (male) and '*clovek*' (man and human), though few Czechs are aware that the word 'Czech' was derived from '*clovek*'.

They may have two words for 'man' but they have umpteen for man's second favourite activity (the first one being liquid, of course). As writer Benjamin Kuras points out:

'The Czech word '*mrd*' for 'bonk' is only one of about 30 words the Czechs have for love-making, depending on the way it is done, speed and duration, the attitude with which it is approached, state of mind, and depth or emotional involvement. A *mrd* would be a hearty down to earth, athletic rather than tender, with full abandon and a lot of yelling, no-nonsense and let's-get-on-with-it approach, not worrying too much about emotional depth of involvement but mutually satisfying, ending in healthy fatigue and a good night's sleep.

Another would be a *hrk*, which is a giggly friendly quickie with someone you are familiar enough with not to have to waste time on foreplay every time. A *drb* is an uninvolved, absent-minded, cynical and loveless act, taking no account of your partner's feel-ings, sort of rabbit-like. All other ways have some vowels, as an expression of something smoother, rounder, gentler, slower, longer, more thoughtful, or more delicious.

If you cannot tell one way from another, you are a *blb*, which is the most frequent Czech word for idiot. The male organ used for the *hrk* is a *brk*, and the jerky motion in which it is done is a *strk*. The finger used for the foreplay is *prst*, and the breast it started on was *prs*. If you were moved to ecstasy, your eyes could weep with a lot of *slz*, and you could be proud of yourself – or *hrd*.'

One word
Greek, Latin and the English language have given mankind a great many universal terms (from 'absti-

nence' to 'web'). This, to the average Czech, is rather extravagant; nations should jealously guard their words and keep them, as much as possible, to themselves.

This is not making excuses, oh no. If the Czechs really wanted to, they could easily join the rank and file and flood the international language babel with their own contributions. To prove their point, they have done it just once: they gave the world the word 'ROBOT'. An artificial word, admittedly, and created some 80 years ago by Czech dramatist Karel Čapek who wanted to describe a humanoid machine, but a worthy one.

66 The Czechs gave the world the word 'ROBOT'. 99

Yes, if the Czechs really wanted... But luckily for the universe, they do not.

One letter

The 14th-century Holy Roman Emperor and Bohemian* King Charles IV had an impressive collection of royal jewels made, including a crown.

* A term that does not mean the country has a 'bohemian' lifestyle. It was the French, centuries ago, who gave the word 'bohem' to gipsy travellers migrating to France from the Balkans and claiming to have come via the Czech lands, a word subsequently applied to those with flair and attitude: students, artists, the unconventional, the unemployable...

The crown was strictly for the heads of the lawful rulers of the Bohemian lands. An old legend says that he who abuses the crown will die a horrible death. The last time in history that this happened, it was Adolf Hitler who did it; and look what happened to him.

However, the real 'jewel' which makes the average Czech inflate with pride is not an item made of gold and precious stones, but a vowel. It's one that looks like an 'r' with a hooklet or a wedge above itself ('ř'). This is a letter that is to all intents and purposes practically unpronounceable. Even Czechs have difficulties with it, even some famous ones – like ex-president and writer Vaclav Havel. Its onomatopoeic sound lies somewhere between "rrr", "shh" and "zzz" and the closest to it is the sound of a circular saw just being switched off.

> **The real 'jewel' which makes the average Czech inflate with pride is not an item made of gold and precious stones, but a vowel.**

To sum it all up: the Czechs gave the world one invention (the *ruchadlo*, and nobody knows what it's for); one writer (Franz Kafka, who wasn't a Czech); one national hero (the Good Soldier Švejk who never existed); one artificial word (robot) and one unpronounceable letter ('ř'). The Czechs therefore are the number ONE in the world. Cheers and bottoms up!

The Authors

Petr Berka demonstrated in front of the guns of Soviet tanks as they entered Czechoslovakia – in his mother's womb. His childhood was like *Happy Days* and *The Fonz*: Very Cool, but at 18, to avoid fighting against Western Imperialism via compulsory military service, he found himself very unwell for years.

In the meantime, he studied biology and anthropology, his graduation thesis being "What do Brits and Germans think about Czechs?" He then began working as a city guide in Prague to explain to foreigners that his compatriots might not be quite as they seem.

Aleš Palán's highest qualification is from driving school, having passed with distinction after only five attempts. Under the communist regime he used his creative forces to the full working as a navvy, acquiring the skills necessary to build a really impressive cottage.

A writer and journalist, his books are based on interviews with prominent Czech personalities. In view of the fact that many of his subjects died during the writing of them, there is an extraordinary interest in his services. Every Czech publisher knows exactly who he should be interviewing next – ideally without delay. Should the reader have any tips, he is more than willing to consider them.

Petr Šťastný, entrepreneur, graphic designer, artist and translator (www.pstastny.eu) claims that his most challenging and enjoyable creative project of recent times has been the transcription of a clutch of *Xenophobe's® Guides* into the Czech language.

As a youngster, he enrolled at art college in the expectation that nude models would be provided. His disillusionment wasn't helped by the Soviet invasion so he decided to do a runner. He put on some slippers and was off, running (and stumbling) from one continent to the next (an idea later copied by Tom Hanks).

After a brief stop-over in Britain that extended to a couple of decades, he returned to Prague in the hope of getting a refund on his slippers. He is still waiting.

The Americans

The American language embraces the bias towards good feelings. Stocks that plummet to half their value aren't losers, they're 'non-performers'. Someone doesn't have a near brush with death; he or she has a 'life-affirming experience'.

The Austrians

As a result of the languages and intelligence of several peoples being gathered into a unity, the Austrians live in several diverse traditions and are thus capable of taking up different positions simultaneously.

The Swiss

Swiss farmers are tough, independent, hard-working, resilient, well-prepared for every kind of natural disaster and above all staunchly conservative. These characteristics have been passed on to Swiss town-dwellers, who go about their day as if they too were farming a lonely mountain cliff.

The English

Tradition, to the English, represents continuity, which must be preserved at all costs. It gives them a sense of permanence in an age of change. Like a well-worn jersey with holes in the sleeves, it's the comfort of the familiar.

The Italians

Italians grow up knowing that they have to be economical with the truth. All other Italians are, so if they didn't play the game they would be at a serious disadvantage. They have to fabricate to keep one step ahead.

The Germans

The Germans strongly disapprove of the irrelevant, the flippant, the accidental. On the whole Germans would prefer to forgo a clever invention rather than admit that creativity is a random and chaotic process.

On the series:

"If I were a cabaret artist or stand up comedian, I'd just get up and read these books to the audience as they would bring the house down." Reviewer of *Het Parool*, Holland

The Aussies:

"One gem of a book. Compulsory reading for anyone interested in visiting Australia or living there. Don't look like a stunned mullet, read the Guide!" Reader from Australia

The Poles:

"A very funny and clever little book. Entertaining, insightful and a lot of fun." Reader from England

The Danes

"A wonderful energetic sense of irony and humour, combined with a deep insight into the Danish culture and mentality. " Reader from Denmark

The Spanish:

"This book is just fantastic and everything it says is true. All the topics are treated with lots of humour and that makes it really enjoyable." Reader from Spain

Xenophobe's® guides

Xenophobe's® lingo learners

66 Speak the lingo by speaking English.99

Ⓞ
Oval Books

5 St John's Buildings Canterbury Crescent London SW9 7QH

The Xenophobe's® Guide series can be bought via Amazon or from **Oval Books** by contacting us directly, or through our web site:

www.ovalbooks.com

Oval Books
5 St John's Buildings
Canterbury Crescent
London SW9 7QH

Payment can be made by cheque (payable to Oval Books), or by credit card*

telephone: +44 (0)20 7733 8585
e-mail: info@ovalbooks.com

Oval Books charges the full cover price for its books (because they're worth it) and £2.00 for postage and packing, but for more than one book (to one address) postage and packing will be FREE.

Xenophobe's® Guides are also available as e-books. Please refer to our web site:

www.ovalbooks.com

*We accept Visa or Mastercard. Orders are dispatched as soon as the card details and mailing address are received. If the mailing address is not the same as the card holder's address it is necessary to give both.

O
Oval Books